Gerry the One-Eared Cat

DAWN BROOKES

Gerry the One-Eared Cat

Don't let the bullies get you down

DAWN BROOKES
Illustrated by Angela Simonovska

OAKWOOD PUBLISHING

Paperback Edition 2018

Kindle Edition 2018

Paperback ISBN: 978-1-9998575-4-7

Cover Illustration Angela Simonovska

To Shona who showed kindness to an elderly one-eared cat

Contents

Chapter 1
Kittens

Early one morning, a black cat named Samantha gave birth to a litter of kittens. There were seven little kittens in total. They were beautiful. Five of the newborns were black and white, one was all black like her mother, and one of them was all white. There were four boys and three girls.

There was only one problem on that happy day. When Samantha went to feed her kittens, she noticed that the white kitten had only one ear. This kitten was also smaller than the rest.

Samantha looked at her kittens and loved them all, especially the tiny little white kitten with only one ear. As she looked at him, she knew that he could have trouble in life. Already, the other kittens were pushing him out of the way, making it hard for him to feed. It wasn't long before they were teasing him about his missing ear.

Soon after they were born, people came to look at the kittens. All of them would be going to new homes.

Adults and children visited the house and they petted and played with all of the cute little kittens, except for the one-eared white kitten. No-one seemed to want a one-eared kitten and they avoided looking at him.

Samantha noticed how his brothers and sisters pushed him out of the way when people came. She also noticed that he stopped running towards the newcomers who entered the house.

"Don't be sad," she said to him. "I love you."

"But no-one wants me, Mum," he meowed.

"Someone will want you, and that will be a very special someone – just like you are a very special kitten."

Samantha knew that her humans, Mr
and Mrs May, could not keep another cat
because they were growing old. Kittens
are very playful and require a lot of
energy. As it was, Mrs May had almost
tripped over the kittens on a number of
occasions.

Mr and Mrs May looked sad, too.
They didn't seem to know what to do
about the one-eared kitten.

Chapter 2
New Homes

All of the kittens had been reserved by different people and they would shortly be going to their new homes. All, that is, apart from the tiny little one-eared white kitten.

The kittens were happy and playful together, but they continued to tease their brother because he looked different. He became more and more withdrawn.

One day, a little girl named Carla came to look at the kittens with her parents. The elderly owners looked sad. They knew that all the kittens were reserved and they feared the family would not want a one-eared kitten.

As soon as they walked in, the little girl ran straight over to the white kitten and stroked him. Samantha was delighted to see this and she watched closely, hoping that her little white kitten would find happiness.

Carla and the kitten played and played. The little girl giggled and the white kitten purred. Finally, Carla looked at her parents.

"Can I have this one, please?"

Mr and Mrs May and Samantha all held their breath.

"Have you noticed that he only has one ear?" her mother asked.

"Yes, Mummy, but why would that matter? He's beautiful and he likes me. I love him."

Carla's parents agreed to buy the kitten and they took him home the following weekend. Samantha was thrilled and she felt her little boy would be content with Carla to look after him.

Chapter 3
Trying to Fit In

When they got home, the little white kitten followed Carla everywhere she went.

"What would you like to call him?" asked her father.

"I think I'll call him Gerry," replied Carla.

Gerry was an extremely happy little kitten.

As Gerry grew into a young cat, he was always pleased when Carla was at home. They would play for hours. Gerry chased little balls that Carla threw for him and he rolled around on the floor for her to tickle him. Carla loved him and he loved her.

The only problem for little Gerry was that Carla had to go to school, and her parents went to work. Each day before they left the house, Gerry was put outside.

He discovered that there were lots of other cats in the area. There was none more beautiful than a cat called Sassy. Sassy was the most popular cat, and Gerry so wanted to be her friend. For weeks, he lay under a hedge, watching the other cats play.

One day he plucked up the courage to approach Sassy, who was surrounded by six other cats. He hesitated because he remembered how his brothers and sisters had always pushed him away.

"Who are you?" asked a big ginger tomcat, gruffly.

"I'm Gerry, I was wondering if I could play with you."

"He's only got one ear," cried a black and white cat, scornfully.

"You're right, Timmy," said a grey cat. "That's just weird!"

Sassy looked at Gerry and then turned her back on him. "Go away, little cat. You look peculiar and you don't fit in here."

Gerry was heartbroken. He walked
away feeling sad. He didn't understand
why no-one liked him just because he
only had one ear. He went back to hiding
under a bush close to his home.

Unfortunately for him, every day was
the same. Gerry gave up trying to join in
with the other cats. Most days, he would
hide in the bushes, feeling very lonely
and isolated, until Carla came home from
school. Once he saw her and observed

how her face lit up when she saw him, he became a happy little cat again.

Sassy still looked beautiful in his eyes, but while he longed to be her friend, he noticed that she was often mean to the other cats too. She was only pleasant when the mood suited her. Each cat tried hard to be part of the group and they seemed happy when they were accepted.

As much as he longed to be accepted too and be part of the group, he felt that it wasn't right to hurt other cats' feelings. Gerry had a kind heart just like his best friend, Carla.

Chapter 4
Withdrawn

As time went by, Gerry became more and more depressed. He spent most of his days feeling gloomy and even found it hard to brighten up when Carla came home.

"Mummy, I think Gerry is unhappy," said Carla one day.

"What makes you think that?" her mother asked.

"He doesn't seem to want to go out in the mornings and his eyes look sad. There's something wrong."

"I'm sure he's fine," said her mother, but Carla was less sure.

Gerry wished he could explain how he felt and how he didn't want to go out in the mornings. All he wanted to do was to stay at home where he felt happy and secure.

Chapter Five
Close Calls

One day, when Gerry decided to go for a walk, he was almost run over by a car because he didn't hear it coming. The car had approached from his left side which was the side where he didn't have an ear. Thankfully, the car driver managed to swerve around and miss him.

"I hate myself," said Gerry out loud. "I wish I had never been born. It's not my fault that I have only one ear. It's just not fair." Gerry was distressed and he felt truly miserable.

Gerry was sitting in the park, feeling sorry for himself, and he didn't hear the sound of something approaching him from his left. By the time he realised he was no longer alone, it was too late – he was staring into the eyes of a gigantic dog! His heart was pounding in his chest. He arched his back and hissed like he had seen other cats do when they felt threatened.

"Oh dear," he said. "I don't want to die. I want to see Carla again."

The back-arching and hissing weren't
working. The dog continued to look at
him, bemused.

"And what makes you think you're
going to die, little cat?"

"Well, you're a dog. Dogs eat cats. I've
heard the other cats speaking about it.
They always run when they see a dog."

"Not everything you hear is true,
little cat. Some dogs don't like cats and

chase them so you do have to be careful. Nevertheless, it is better to judge what you see, rather than what you hear. Some cats don't like each other, either. Have you never seen a cat fight? Do all cats kill birds? Do you?"

The large black and white dog sat down.

"I would never do that," said Gerry, horrified at the thought.

"Well, there you are, then. Not everything you hear is true. I was told when I was a pup that all cats kill birds. I learned, though, that not every creature behaves in the way they are presumed to. Not everything bigger than you is dangerous; sometimes, small things can harm you. You just need to learn what is really dangerous and what isn't."

"How will I learn that?"

The wise old dog looked at Gerry and sighed. "You will learn how to judge that as you grow up. I can see that you are still a very young cat."

At that moment, Gerry saw that the dog had a shiny white circle in one of her eyes.

"What's wrong with your eye?" he asked.

"I can't see out of that side," replied the dog. "I used to be able to, but now I can't. I'm a lot older than you – things wear out as you get older."

"Does it bother you?" asked Gerry.

"No, I've got used to it, and my other eye is perfectly good. Why should it bother me?"

Gerry looked sad. "I only have one ear," he said miserably.

"So I see, but why should that worry you so much? You have a good ear, don't you?"

"None of the other cats like me because of it. I'm different. They tease me about my ear whenever they see me."

"If the other cats don't like you because you're different, they are shallow. They are probably not worth knowing anyway. You need to find

friends who will accept you just as you are.”

“But I like one of the girl cats.” Gerry looked down at his paws glumly.

“Mm, and I bet she is the most popular cat in the area.”

“How did you know that?”

“It’s always the same; everyone wants to follow the in-crowd. What I do know, little cat, is that being popular doesn’t always mean being kind.” The wise old dog looked at Gerry. “Is this cat kind?”

“Not always, no.”

“Is she kind to the other cats who are her friends?”

"Not always." Gerry looked even more gloomy.

"What are the other cats like when they are with her?"

"They're mean too."

"And what about when they are not with her?"

"Some of them are still mean, but some of them are nicer." Gerry was starting to understand what the old dog meant.

"There you have it," said the dog, kindly. "If she did like you, and you became a part of that group, you would have to become mean and nasty to stay part of it, especially when you were with her. Would you be comfortable with that?"

"No, I don't suppose I would."

"Then why would you want to be her friend?"

"When you put it like that, I guess I don't know. I was just attracted to her because everybody likes her, and I like her. I want to belong; I'm lonely."

"Little cat, take it from an old dog. You will find friends when you stop trying too hard. When you stop wanting to be part of a crowd of bullies, you will find friends. Maybe you're looking in the wrong places. Who would have thought that you and I could be friends? But we can be when we stop looking at our differences. We can talk, like we are doing now."

"I had never considered being friends with a dog before," replied Gerry, realising that he too had his prejudices. "What's your name?"

"My name is Issie. I live with an old cat at home. She's black, and I'm pleased to say, she is happy to be friends with a dog who can only use one eye."

"I'm Gerry. Will we meet again? I'd like to be your friend."

"I expect we will, Gerry, but I need to go back to my humans now. They are calling me. Bye for now." With that, the old dog walked away.

Gerry felt so much better inside.

Chapter 6
Belonging

From that day on, Gerry would ignore the jibes he got from the cats in the street.

Whenever he heard Sassy and the other cats shouting, "Hey, there's one-ear again. Wonder where he's been", instead of feeling sad and dejected, Gerry felt calm and happy. He didn't want to be a

part of their group. He held his head up
high and walked past, ignoring them.

When Carla came home from school on the day he first met Issie, Gerry ran to her. He was happy again. He knew that she would love him, no matter how different he looked. He realised it was more important to know he was loved than it was to be part of a crowd.

Gerry no longer dreaded going out in the mornings. He discovered that he could make other friends. They didn't have to be cats.

He made friends with the birds. Once they realised he wasn't going to harm them, they would come and sing to him. One friendly robin would even land on his head and sing. Gerry purred and relaxed in the sunlight, enjoying his garden.

He made friends with a squirrel who tried to bring him nuts.

"Sorry, I don't eat those," he said. "But I will guard them for you, if you like?"

"Yes please," said the squirrel.

He often met with his friendly old dog friend, Issie. She introduced him to another dog, named Bracken.

"You have a white patch in your eye, just like Issie," Gerry said.

"Yes, I can't see very well these days," the brown and white dog replied. "I can smell for miles, though, so I always know where I am."

"That's clever," said Gerry, impressed.

Gerry realised that you don't have to
be with your own kind to have friends,
and that looking different wasn't a bad
thing at all. His new friends accepted
him for who he was. They didn't even
mention his missing ear, so he stopped
noticing it too. He even learned that the
one ear he did have could do the work of
two. The hearing in his left ear was

sharp, and he was able to use his eyes and his sense of smell to detect danger.

Gerry was much happier now he had real friends.

Chapter 7
Showing Kindness

Gerry was on his way home one day when he saw a cat who didn't normally speak to him lying on her doorstep, all alone and looking sad.

"What's the matter?" he asked.

"Sassy and the others have told me to go away. They don't want to be my friends any more."

"Why?"

"Because I said I was fed up with being mean and nasty. I told them I didn't want to fight with other cats, and I didn't want to chase birds."

"I think that's a brave thing to have said. I'm pleased you don't want to chase birds. I have lots of friends who are birds." Gerry continued, "Do you want to meet them?"

"I've always been mean to you. Why would you want me to come with you?" She looked suspicious.

"Because if I had been accepted as part of that group, I would've been mean too. I learned that lesson from an old dog.

She taught me new tricks. She taught me that love is the most important thing. I am very happy. I have a lovely human called Carla and lots of friends. You'll be my first cat friend, though. What is your name?"

"My name is Misty," said the cat, narrowing her eyes at Gerry to show him that she would very much like to be his friend.

Gerry and Misty became great friends
and went everywhere together. They
learned that diversity meant accepting
differences and they became wonderful
cats as a result. They laughed and joked
together and had so many friends.

They never missed the crowd that
seemed to get ever more miserable as
they grew older. They were always
fighting and moaning, and Gerry thought
it was a sad way to live. He was thankful
that his one ear had prevented him from
being a part of that group.

Gerry couldn't have been happier. He
realised that when Carla chose to take
him home with her on that wonderful
day, she had not looked at his
appearance. She had looked at him for
who he was, and for that he would be
forever grateful.

Letter from the author

Dear Children,

I do hope that you have enjoyed reading about Gerry.

As you can see from Gerry's story, it is important to think about the feelings of others when making friends. It is okay to be different, and when all people realise that we will live in a much kinder world.

The inspiration for this story came from my friend's twenty-three year old daughter who adopted an elderly cat with one ear from the RSPCA. That cat, also called Gerry, arrived at the centre with four other cats. All of the other cats were given homes but no one wanted the one-eared cat who was also very old. My friend's daughter has a very kind heart, just like Carla in this story and I can imagine that she would have done the exact same thing when she was a young girl.

Gerry discovered that he could make friends with creatures that were different to him. I hope that you discover that too. Be kind to people who are different and be kind to animals and nature.

Dawn Brookes

Other Books by Dawn Brookes

Books for Children

Ava & Oliver's Bonfire Night Adventure
Ava & Oliver's Christmas Nativity Adventure
Boats & Ships A to Z
Danny the Caterpillar
Jesus feeds a big crowd!
Jesus heals a man on a stretcher

Memoirs

Hurry up Nurse: memoirs of nurse training in the 1970s
Hurry up Nurse 2: London calling

Coming Soon

Book 2 in the Rachel Prince Mystery Series
Deadly Cruise
Book 3 in the Hurry up Nurse Series
Hurry up Midwife

Keep up to date with what Dawn is writing::
https://www.dawnbrookespublishing.com.
https://www.facebook.com/dawnbrookespublishing
/
If you have enjoyed this book please leave an
honest review on Amazon or any other platform
that you use.

www.ingramcontent.com/pod-product-compliance
Lightning Source LLC
Chambersburg PA
CBHW051719050726
47598CB00003B/966